MW00637904

CogAT® Screening Form
Practice Test
GRADE 2
LEVEL 8

Practice Questions from the CogAT Form 7 / Form 8 Analogies Sections: Verbal/Picture Analogies, Number Analogies, & Figure Matrices

Written and Edited by:
Gifted and Talented Test Preparation Team

ISBN: 978-1-948255-87-5

Origins Publications
New York, NY, USA

Email:info@originspublications.com

Origins Publications

We help students develop their higher-order thinking skills while also improving their chances of admission into gifted and accelerated-learner programs.

Our goal is to unleash and nurture the genius in every student. We do this by offering educational and test prep materials that are fun, challenging and provide a sense of accomplishment.

Please contact us with any questions.

info@originspublications.com

Contents

Part 1: Introduction to the CogAT® Screening Form

This book offers an overview of the types of questions on the CogAT® Level 8 Screening Form, test-taking strategies to improve performance, sample questions, and a full-length CogAT Screening Form practice test that students can use to assess their knowledge and practice their test-taking skills.

Who Takes this Test?

The CogAT Level 8 Screening Form is a test that is often used as an expedient yet reliable assessment tool or admissions test in Grade 2 for entry into 3rd grade of gifted and talented (GATE) programs and highly-competitive schools.

What is the Difference Between the CogAT® and the CogAT® Screening Form?

The CogAT Screening Form is a shorter version of the full length CogAT Form 7. The Screening Form contains only the analogies section of each battery: picture/verbal analogies, number analogies, and figure matrices.

Some schools prefer the CogAT Screening Form, as the test offers a quality evaluation with a shorter administration time than the complete CogAT.

When Does the Test Take Place?

This depends on the school district you reside in or want to attend. Check with the relevant school/district to learn more about test dates and the application/ registration process.

CogAT® Level 8 Screening Form Overview

The CogAT® is a group-administered test that features only the analogies section of each of the three independent 'batteries': Verbal, Quantitative, and Nonverbal. It is designed to assess learned reasoning in these three areas, which experts believe are the areas most closely linked to academic achievement.

The CogAT® covers topics that students may not see in school, so kids will need to think a little differently in order to do well. A student's stress management and time management skills are also tested during the exam.

Length

Students take about 30 minutes to complete the test.

Format

The test is a black and white picture-based exam. The test is made up of 54 multiple choice questions.

Test Sections

Picture Analogies: 18 questions

Students are provided with two pictures that form a pair, as well as a third picture. From the answer choices, the student must select the picture that goes with the third provided image.

Number Analogies: 18 questions

Students are given a 2x2 matrix with one empty cell. The student must determine the relationship between the two images in the top row, the picture that has the same relationship with the image on the bottom row.

Figure Matrices: 18 questions

Students are given a 2x2 matrix with the image missing in one cell. Students must determine the relationship between the two spatial forms in the bottom row.

Part 2: How to Use this Book

The CogAT® Screening Form is an important test and the more a student is familiar with the questions on the exam, the better she will fare when taking the test.

This book will help your child get used to the format and content of the test so s/he will be adequately prepared and feel confident on test day.

Inside this book, you will find:

• Sample question for each question type on the test and teaching tips to help your child approach each question type strategically and with confidence.

• Full-length CogAT® Level 8 Screening Form practice test.

• Access to bonus CHALLENGE practice questions online for the **full-length** CogAT at **https://originstutoring.lpages.co/cogat-8-challenge-questions/**

Part 3. Test Prep Tips and Strategies

Firstly, and most importantly, commit to make the test preparation process a stress-free one. A student's ability to keep calm and focused in the face of challenge is a quality that will benefit her throughout her academic life.

Be prepared for difficult questions from the get-go! There will be a certain percentage of questions that are very challenging for all children. It is key to encourage students to use all strategies available when faced with challenging questions. And remember that a student can get quite a few questions wrong and still do very well on the test.

Before starting the practice test, go through the sample questions and read the teaching tips provided at the beginning of the book. They will help you guide your student as he or she progresses through the practice test.

The following strategies may also be useful as you help your child prepare:

Before You Start

Find a quiet, comfortable spot to work free of distractions.

Tell your student you will be doing some fun activities, and that this is an opportunity for you to spend some enjoyable time together.

Show your student how to perform the simple technique of shading (and erasing) bubbles.

During Prep

If your child is challenged by a question, ask your child to explain why he or she chose a specific answer. If the answer was incorrect, this will help you identify where your child is stumbling. If the answer was correct, asking your child to articulate her reasoning aloud will help reinforce the concept.

Encourage your child to carefully consider all the answer options before selecting one. Tell her there is only ONE correct answer.

If your child is stumped by a question, she or he can use the process of elimination. First, encourage your child to eliminate obviously wrong answers to narrow down the answer choices. If your child is still in doubt after using this technique, tell him or her to guess as there are no points deducted for wrong answers.

Review all the questions your student answered incorrectly, and explain to your student why the answer is incorrect. Have your student attempt these questions again a few days later to see if he now understands the concept.

Encourage your student to do her best, but take plenty of study breaks. Start with 10-15 minute sessions. Your student will perform best if she views these activities as fun and engaging, not as exercises to be avoided.

Picture Analogies Sample Question and Tips

There are 18 Picture Analogies questions in the CogAT® Level 8 Screening Form.

SAMPLE QUESTION:

Which image best fits in the box with the question mark?

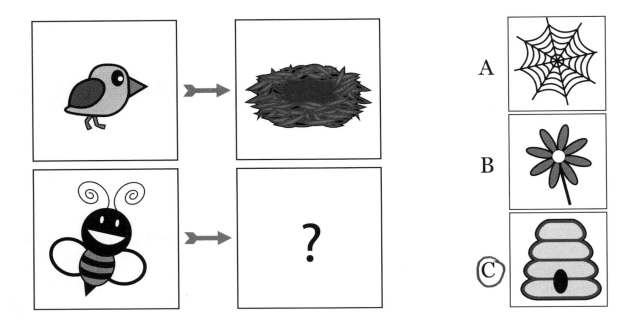

Correct Answer: C

Answer Explanation

In the top row, there are two figures that go together in the sense that a bird's home is a nest, or a bird lives in a nest.

Look at the bottom row. Your child needs to find the picture among the answer options that fits best in the question mark box on the bottom row. The correct choice has the same relationship with the picture on the left on the bottom row as the two pictures in the top row have with each other.

Option A is incorrect because a bee's home is not a web.

Option B is also incorrect as a bee's home is not a flower, even though bees like flowers.

Option C is correct because, just like a bird's home is a nest, a bee's home is a hive.

TEACHING TIPS

- To master picture analogies, a student needs to have general background knowledge, a good visual vocabulary, and an understanding/recognition of the following relationships:

    → Object/function (or reverse: function/object)

    → Agent (person or animal)/location, (or reverse: location/agent (person or animal)

    → Agent (person or animal)/object, (or reverse: object/agent (person or animal)

    → Agent (person or animal)/action, (or reverse: action/ agent (person or animal)

    → Familial -- having to do with family.

- As often as possible, incorporate discussions about similarities, differences, and relationships between words into your everyday conversation with your student. Help your student begin thinking about how different words and concepts are connected to one another.

- When answering practice questions, teach your student to determine the relationship between the first pair of pictures before looking at the answer choices. Once your student determines the relationship between the first pair, she can then look at the choices to find the pair with the exact same relationship.

Figure Matrices

There are 18 Figure Matrices questions in the CogAT® Level 8 Screening Form.

SAMPLE QUESTION:

Look at the shapes in the boxes on top. These shapes go together in a certain way. Which answer choice belongs where the question mark is?

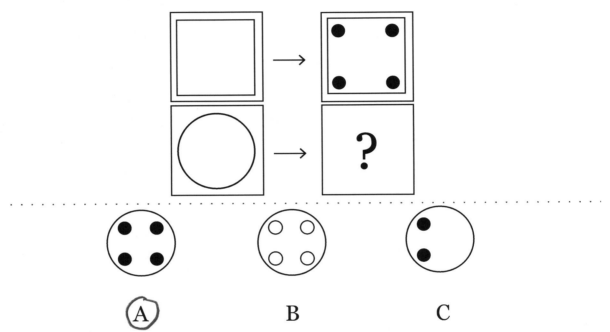

Correct Answer: A

Answer Explanation

In the top row, there are two figures that go together in a certain way. They go together in the sense that as the figure moves from left box to right box, it stays the same shape (a square) but adds four black circles inside.

Your child needs to find the figure among the answer options that fits best in the question mark box on the bottom row. The correct choice will have the same relationship with the figure on the bottom row that the figures in the top row have with each other.

Option B is incorrect because, although the figure is the same shape as the figure on the bottom row, the inside circles that are added are white. Option C is incorrect because, although the figure is the same shape as the figure on the bottom row, only two black inside circles are added. Option A is correct as the figure has the same shape (circle) as the figure on the bottom row and it has four black circles inside.

TEACHING TIPS

- Make sure your student knows key concepts that come up in these types of questions, including geometric concepts such as rotational symmetry, line symmetry, parts of a whole.

- If your student is finding these items difficult, encourage her to discover the pattern by isolating one element (e.g: outer shape, inner shape/s) and identify how it changes:

  → Ask: Is the color/shading of the element changing as it moves?

  → Ask: Is the element changing positions as it moves? Does it move up or down? Clockwise or counter-clockwise? Does it end up in the opposite (mirror) position?

  → Ask: Does the element disappear or increase in number as it moves along the row? Does it get bigger or smaller?

- Encourage your student to make a prediction for the missing object and compare the description with the answer choices.

Number Analogies

There are 18 Number Analogies questions in the CogAT® Level 8 Screening Form.

SAMPLE QUESTION

Which image best fits in the box with the question mark?

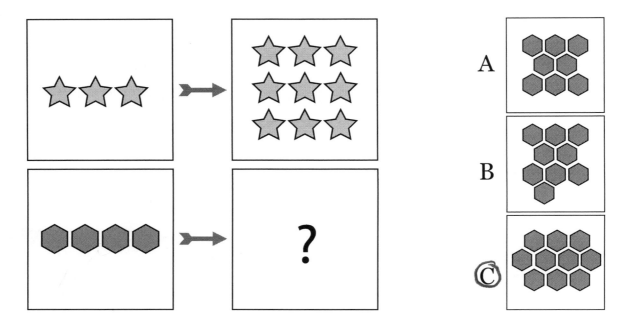

Correct answer: C

Answer Explanation

In the top row, there are two pictures that go together. As we move from the left picture to the picture on the right, the 3 stars become 9 stars. This means that 6 stars have been added to the 3 stars to make 9 stars.

Your child needs to find the picture among the answer options that best fits in the question mark box. The correct choice has the same relationship with the picture on the left on the bottom row as the two pictures in the top row have with each other.

The bottom row picture shows 4 hexagons. To match the relationship in the top row, your child needs to add 6 hexagons to the 4 hexagons in the first box to give a total of 10 hexagons.

Option C is therefore correct as the picture shows 10 hexagons.

TEACHING TIPS

- Your child is probably not accustomed to completing number matrices, so it is important to frequently expose him to this question type in order to build confidence and familiarity.

- Make sure your child has an understanding/recognition of the following relationships:
  - → Part/whole (or reverse: whole/part)
  - → Changes in quantity
  - → Changes in size.

- Consider modeling how to approach solving a number matrix by "thinking aloud" as you work through a question with your child.

- Work with your child on basic mathematical concepts (see teaching tips for Number Puzzles).

CogAT® Level 8 Screening Form Practice Test

Picture Analogies
Practice Questions

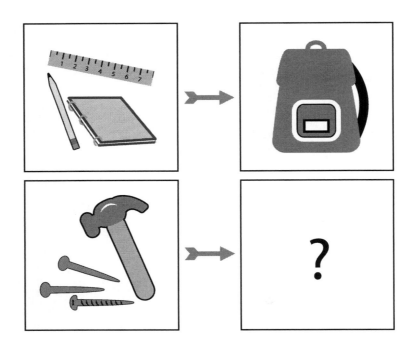

Picture Analogies

Which image best fits in the box with the question mark?

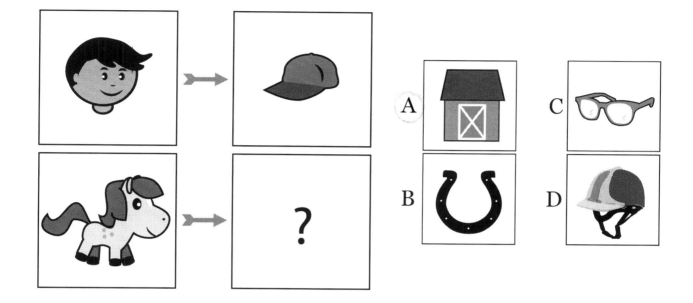

Which image best fits in the box with the question mark?

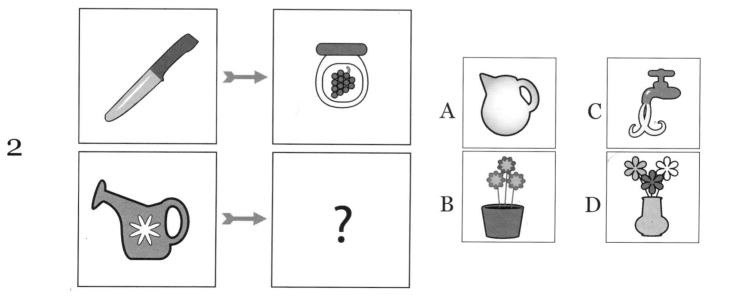

Picture Analogies

Which image best fits in the box with the question mark?

3

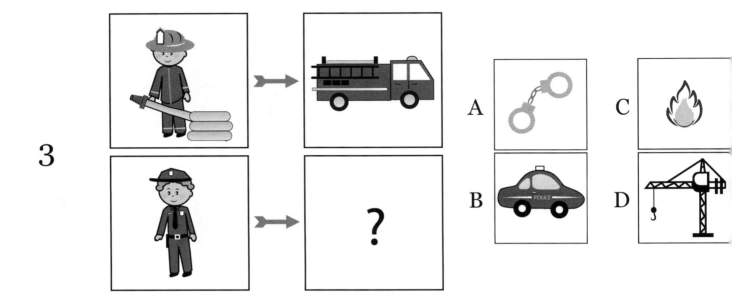

Which image best fits in the box with the question mark?

4

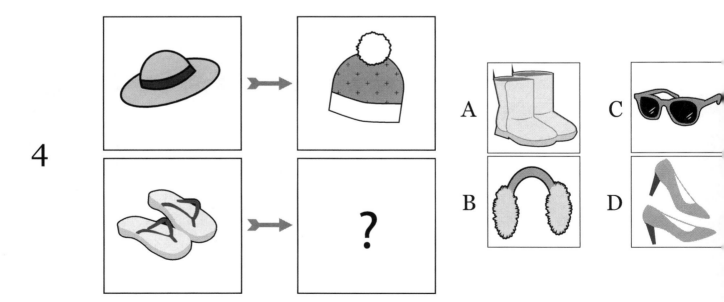

CogAT Level 8 Screening Form Test Prep Book

Picture Analogies

Which image best fits in the box with the question mark?

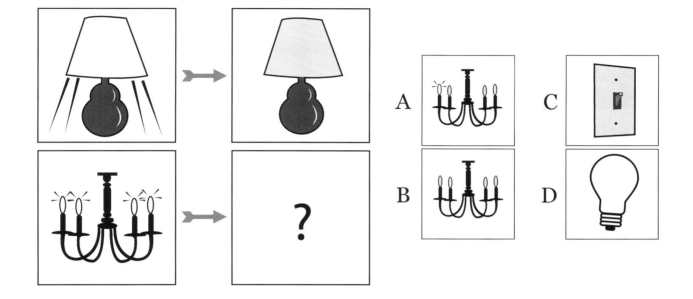

5

Which image best fits in the box with the question mark?

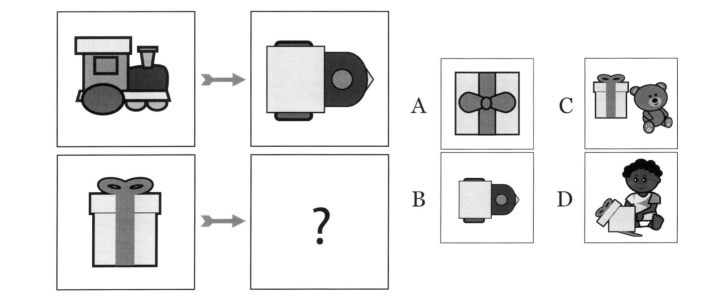

6

Picture Analogies

Which image best fits in the box with the question mark?

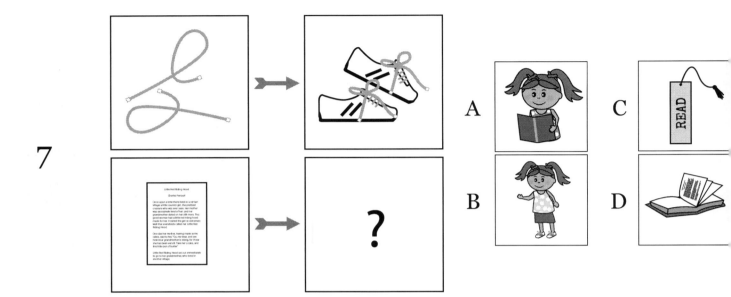

Which image best fits in the box with the question mark?

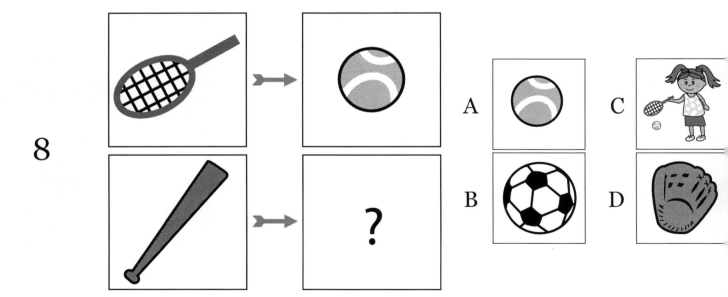

Picture Analogies

Which image best fits in the box with the question mark?

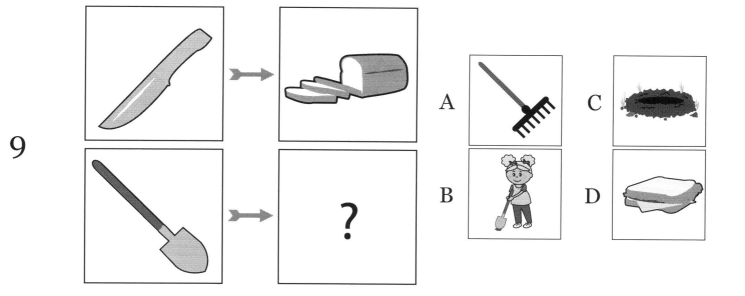

Which image best fits in the box with the question mark?

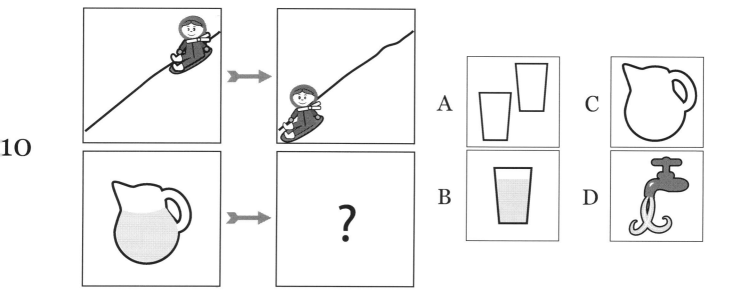

Picture Analogies

Which image best fits in the box with the question mark?

Which image best fits in the box with the question mark?

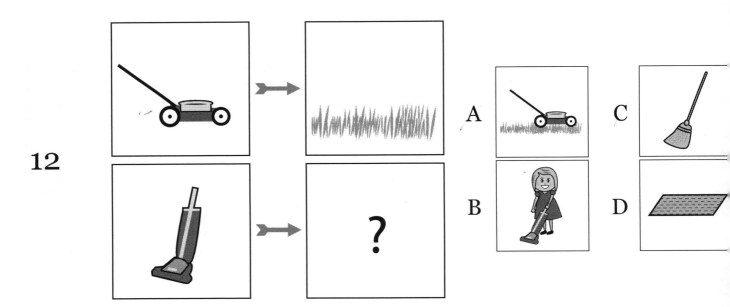

CogAT Level 8 Screening Form Test Prep Book

Picture Analogies

Which image best fits in the box with the question mark?

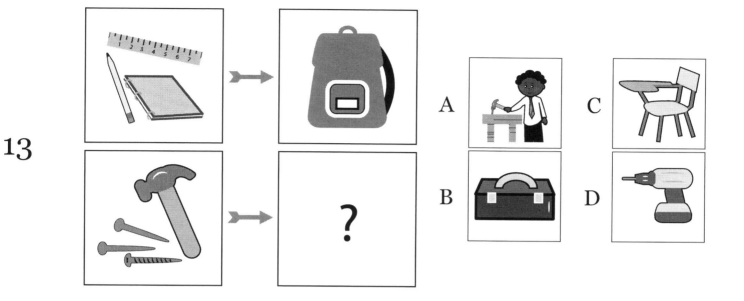

13

Which image best fits in the box with the question mark?

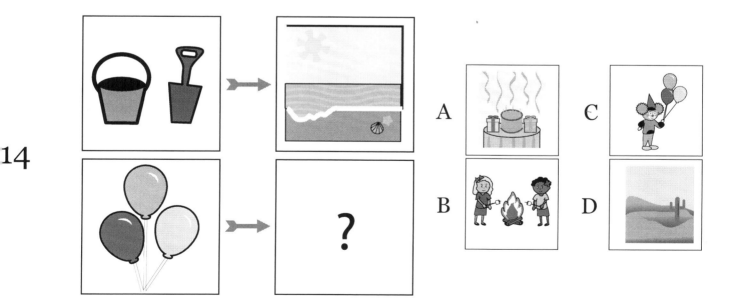

14

Picture Analogies

Which image best fits in the box with the question mark?

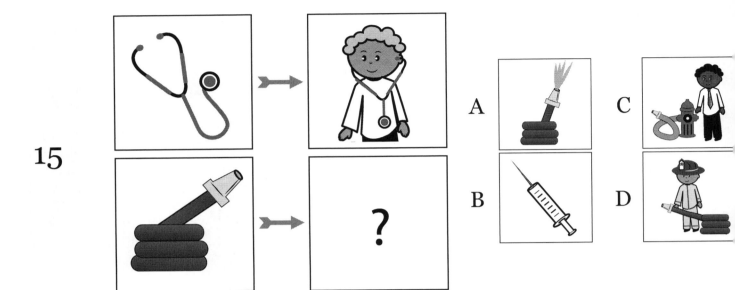

Which image best fits in the box with the question mark?

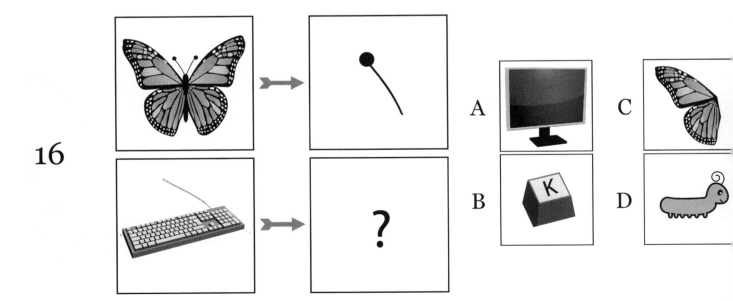

Picture Analogies

Which image best fits in the box with the question mark?

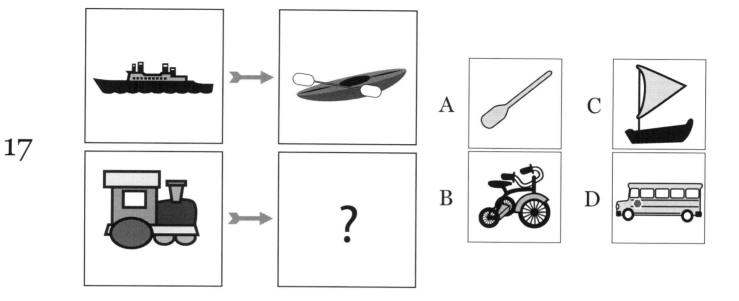

17

Which image best fits in the box with the question mark?

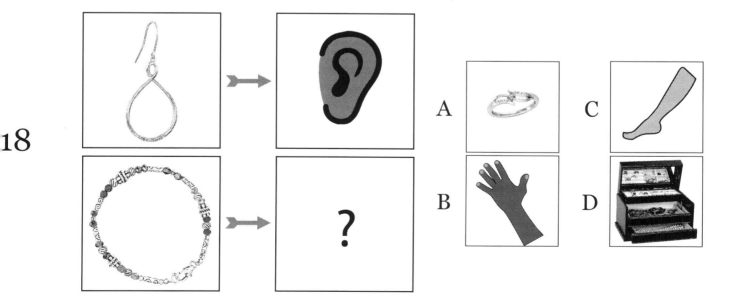

18

Figure Matrices
Practice Questions

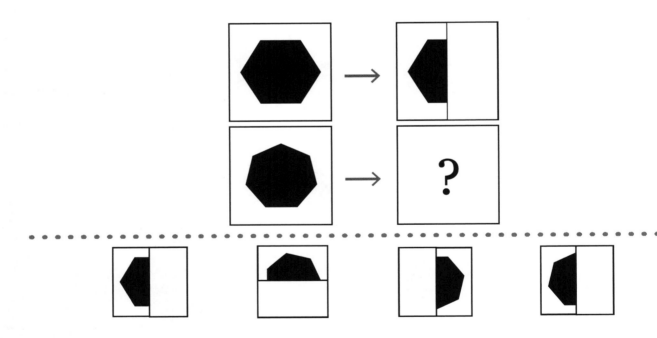

Figure Matrices

Look at the shapes in the boxes on top. These shapes go together in a certain way. Which shape belongs where the question mark is?

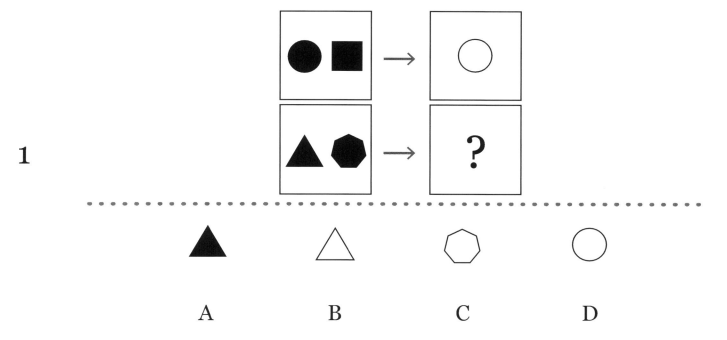

1

Look at the shapes in the boxes on top. These shapes go together in a certain way. Which shape belongs where the question mark is?

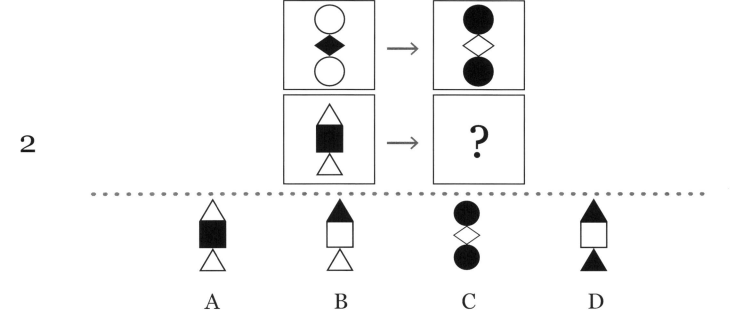

2

Figure Matrices

Look at the shapes in the boxes on top. These shapes go together in a certain way. Which shape belongs where the question mark is?

3

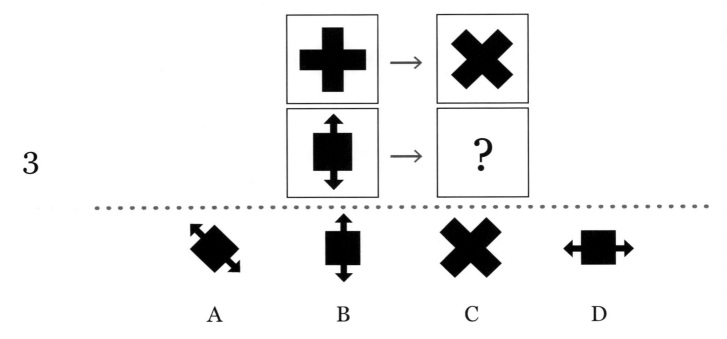

Look at the shapes in the boxes on top. These shapes go together in a certain way. Which shape belongs where the question mark is?

4

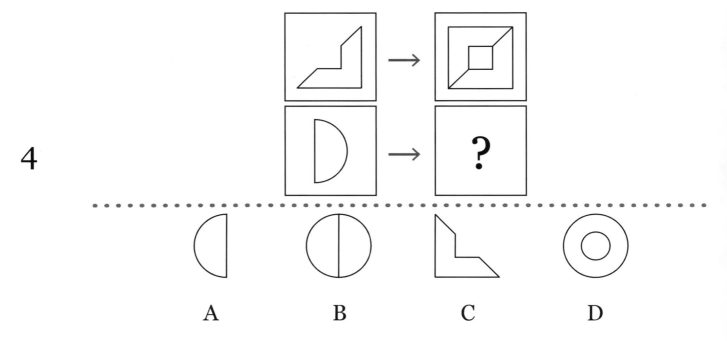

Figure Matrices

Look at the shapes in the boxes on top. These shapes go together in a certain way. Which shape belongs where the question mark is?

5

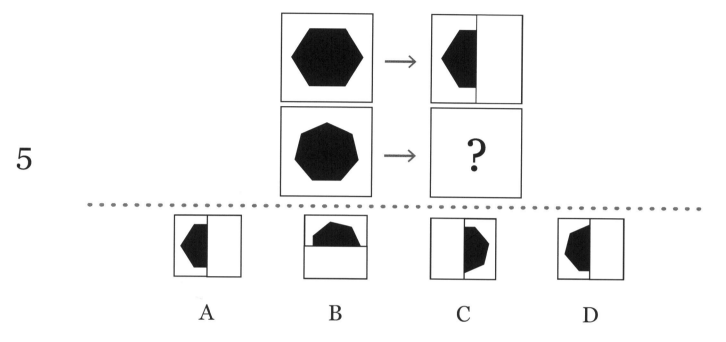

A   B   C   D

Look at the shapes in the boxes on top. These shapes go together in a certain way. Which shape belongs where the question mark is?

6

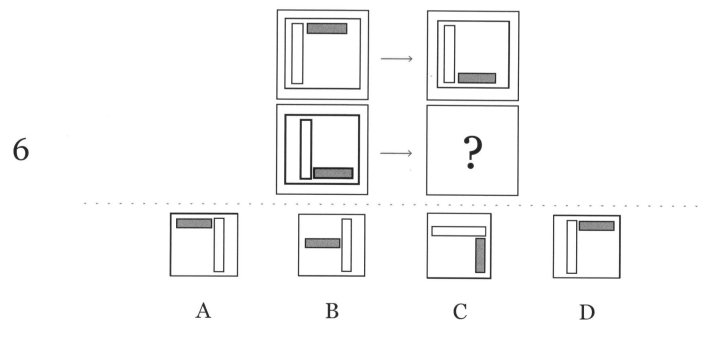

A   B   C   D

Figure Matrices

Look at the shapes in the boxes on top. These shapes go together in a certain way. Which shape belongs where the question mark is?

7

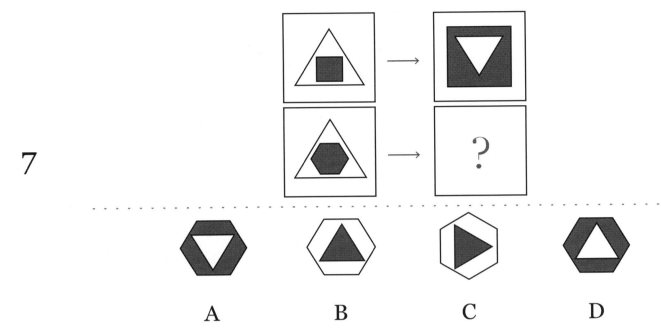

Look at the shapes in the boxes on top. These shapes go together in a certain way. Which shape belongs where the question mark is?

8

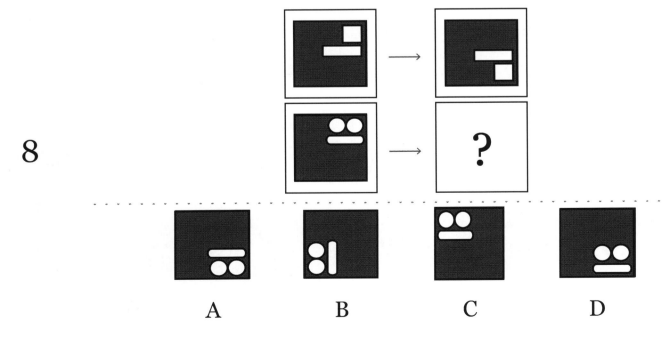

CogAT Level 8 Screening Form Test Prep Book

Figure Matrices

Look at the shapes in the boxes on top. These shapes go together in a certain way. Which shape belongs where the question mark is?

9

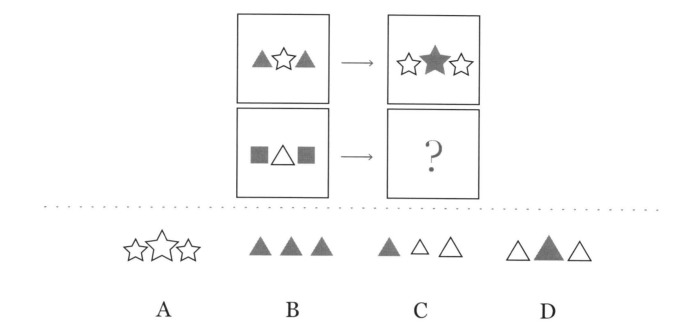

A   B   C   D

Look at the shapes in the boxes on top. These shapes go together in a certain way. Which shape belongs where the question mark is?

10

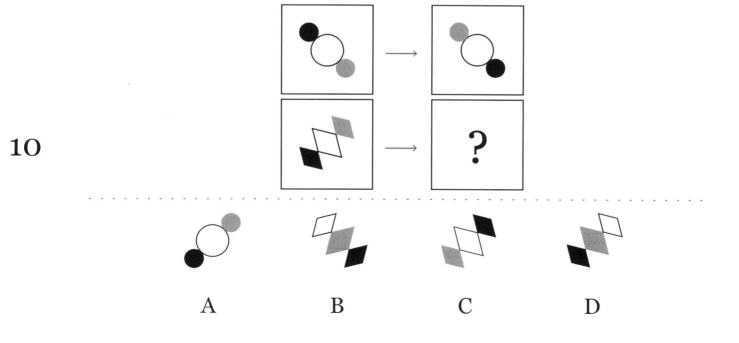

A   B   C   D

Look at the shapes in the boxes on top. These shapes go together in a certain way. Which shape belongs where the question mark is?

11

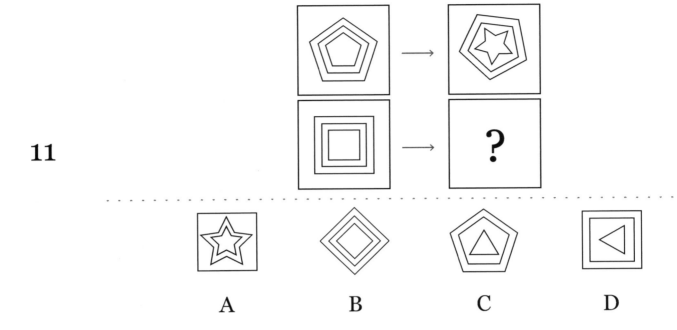

A   B   C   D

Look at the shapes in the boxes on top. These shapes go together in a certain way. Which shape belongs where the question mark is?

12

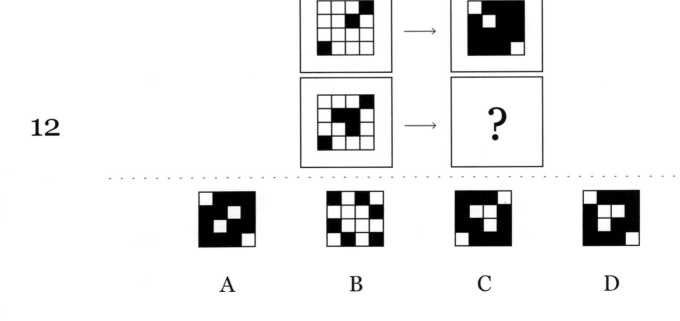

A   B   C   D

Figure Matrices

Look at the shapes in the boxes on top. These shapes go together in a certain way. Which shape belongs where the question mark is?

13

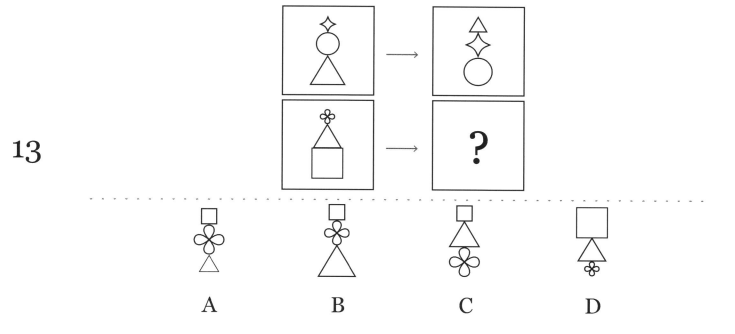

A	B	C	D

Look at the shapes in the boxes on top. These shapes go together in a certain way. Which shape belongs where the question mark is?

14

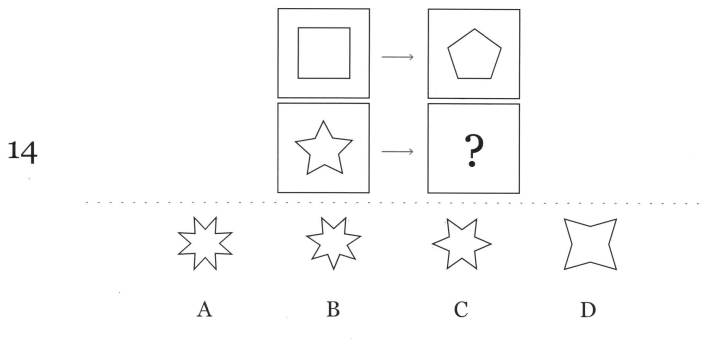

A	B	C	D

Look at the shapes in the boxes on top. These shapes go together in a certain way. Which shape belongs where the question mark is?

15

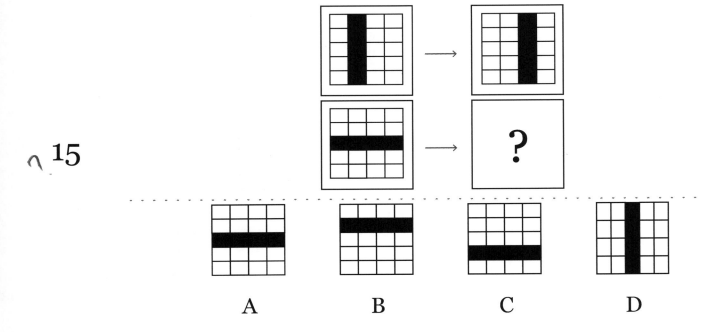

A   B   C   D

Look at the shapes in the boxes on top. These shapes go together in a certain way. Which shape belongs where the question mark is?

16

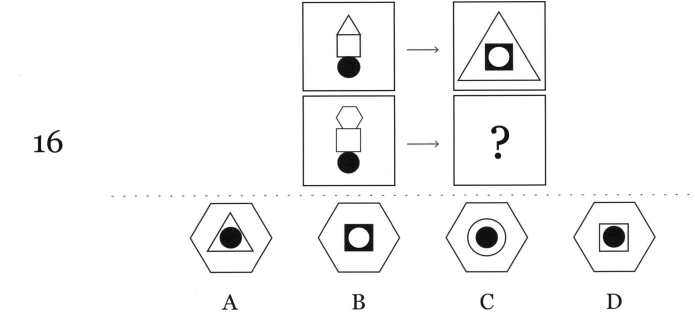

A   B   C   D

Figure Matrices

Look at the shapes in the boxes on top. These shapes go together in a certain way. Which shape belongs where the question mark is?

17

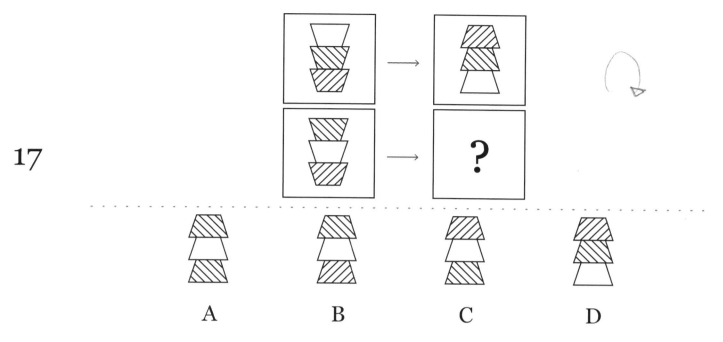

A   B   C   D

Look at the shapes in the boxes on top. These shapes go together in a certain way. Which shape belongs where the question mark is?

18

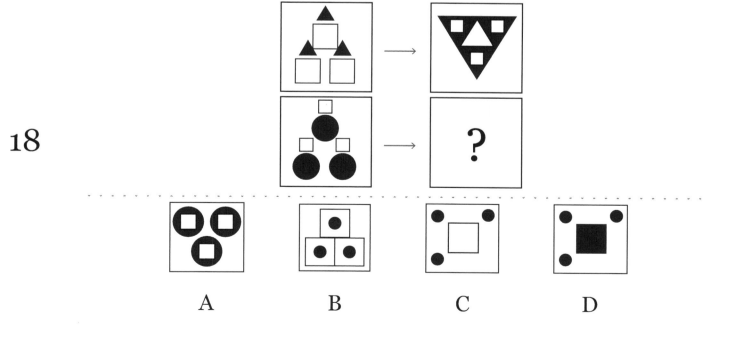

A   B   C   D

Number Analogies
Practice Questions

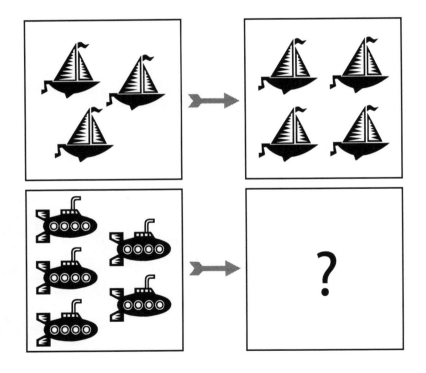
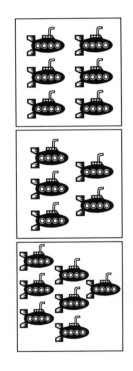

Number Analogies

Which image best fits in the box with the question mark?

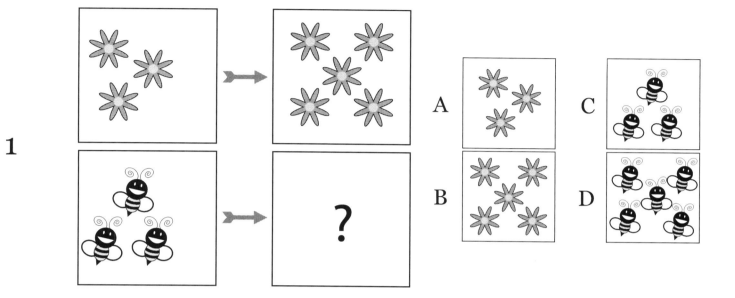

Which image best fits in the box with the question mark?

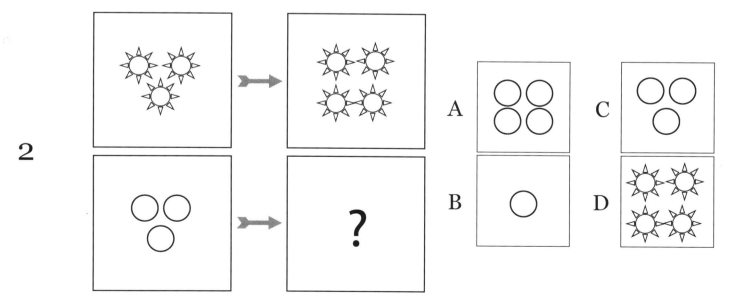

Number Analogies

Which image best fits in the box with the question mark?

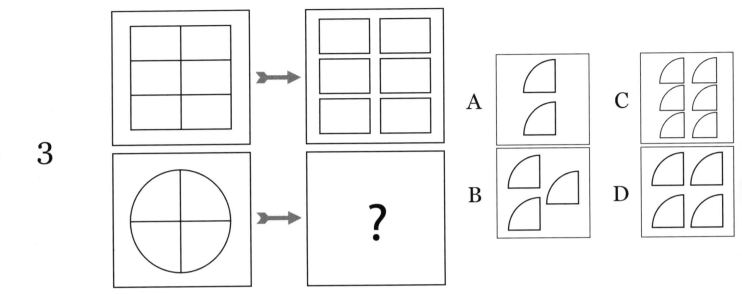

Which image best fits in the box with the question mark?

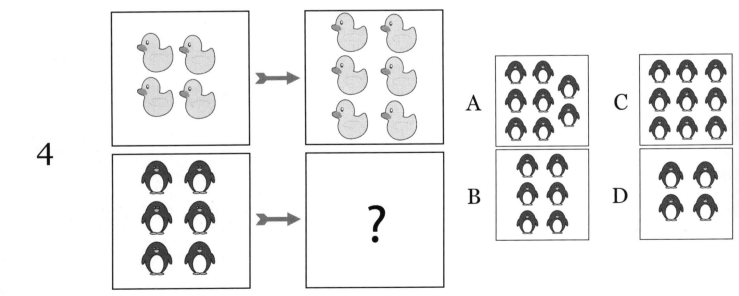

Number Analogies

Which image best fits in the box with the question mark?

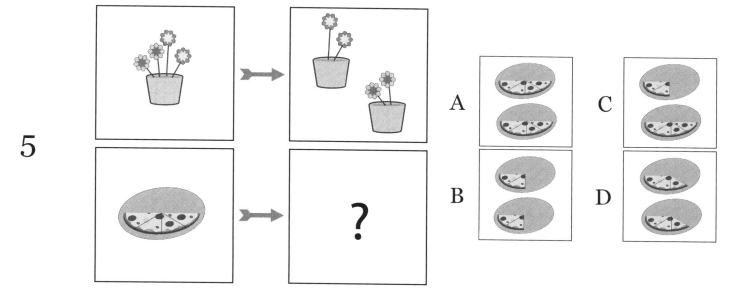

Which image best fits in the box with the question mark?

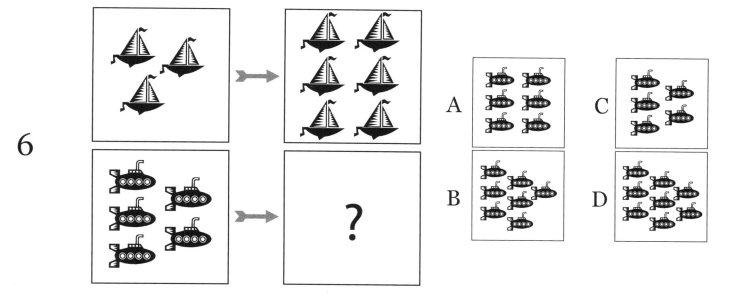

Number Analogies

Which image best fits in the box with the question mark?

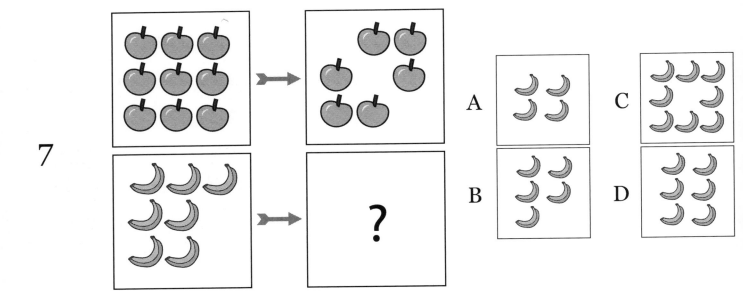

Which image best fits in the box with the question mark?

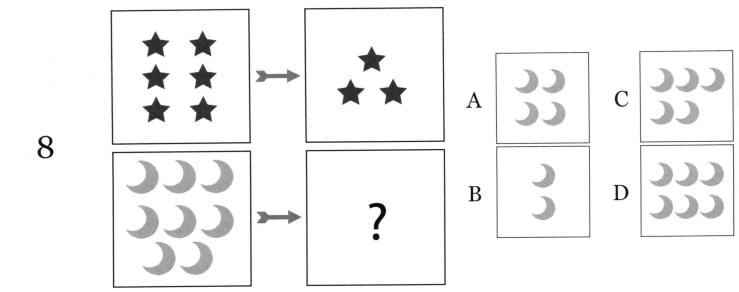

CogAT Level 8 Screening Form Test Prep Book

Number Analogies

Which image best fits in the box with the question mark?

9

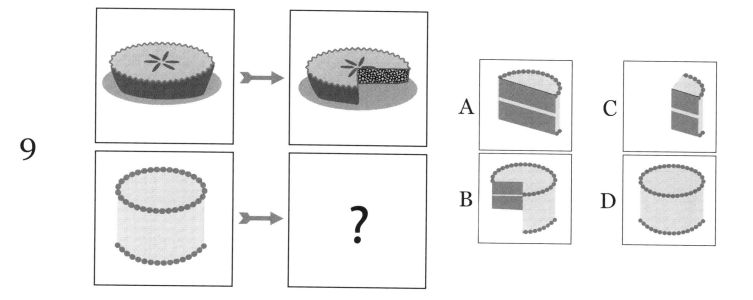

Which image best fits in the box with the question mark?

10

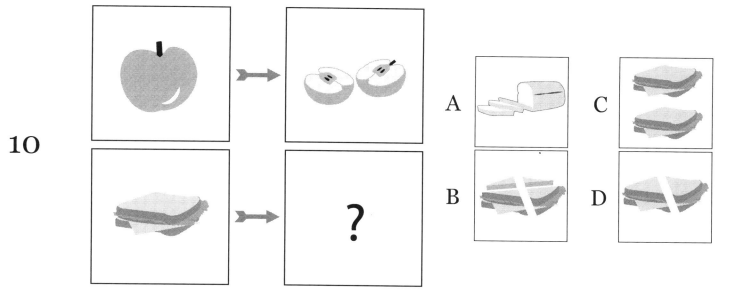

Number Analogies

Which image best fits in the box with the question mark?

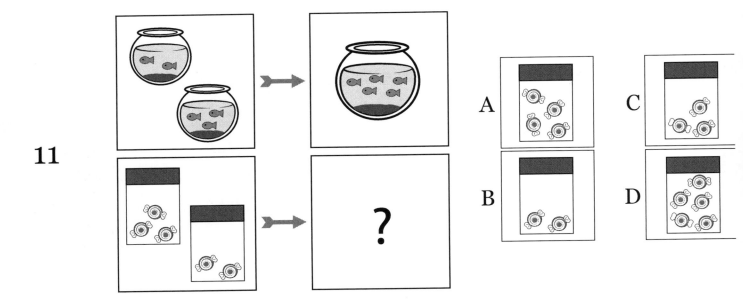

11

Which image best fits in the box with the question mark?

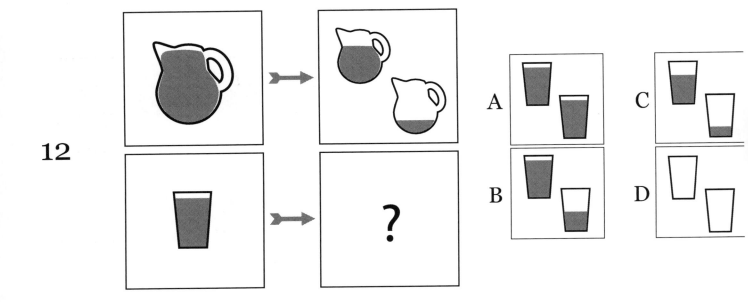

12

Number Analogies

Which image best fits in the box with the question mark?

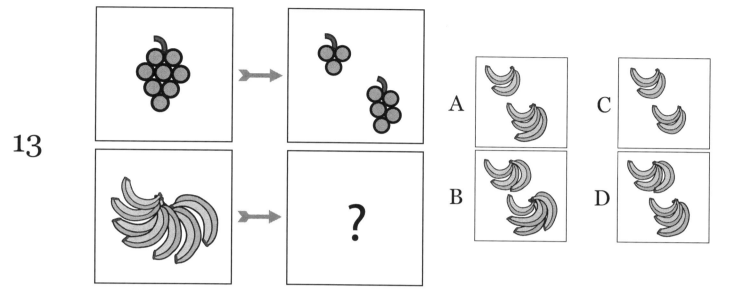

13

Which image best fits in the box with the question mark?

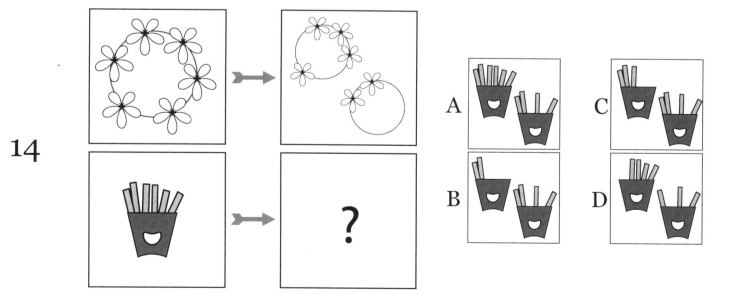

14

Number Analogies

Which image best fits in the box with the question mark?

15

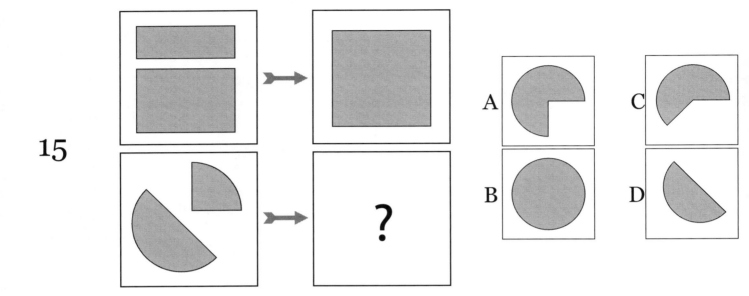

Which image best fits in the box with the question mark?

16

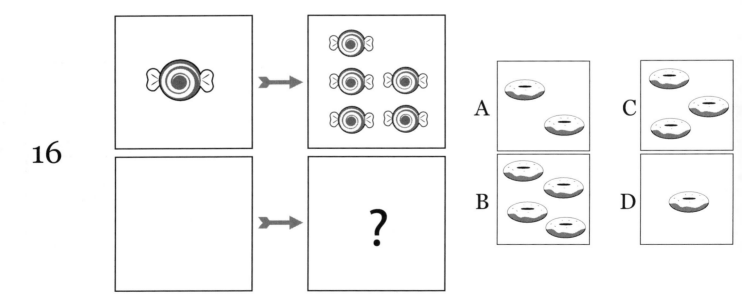

Number Analogies

Which image best fits in the box with the question mark?

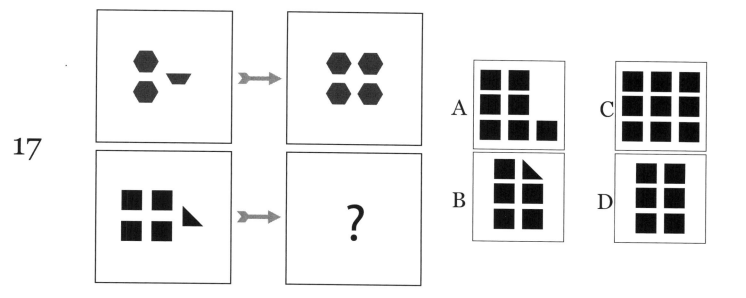

17

Which image best fits in the box with the question mark?

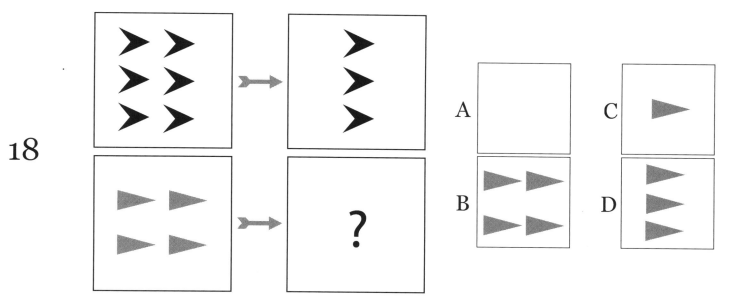

18

Test Answers
& Bubble Sheets

CogAT® Picture Analogies Answers

Number	Answer	Explanation
		Picture Analogies
1	B	
2	B	
3	B	
4	A	
5	B	
6	A	
7	D	
8	A	
9	C	
10	C	
11	A	
12	D	
13	B	
14	A	
15	D	
16	B	
17	B	
18	B	

CogAT® Figure Matrices Answers

Number	Answer	Explanation
		Figure Matrices
1	B	
2	D	
3	A	Figure moves quarter turn to left.
4	B	
5	D	
6	D	
7	A	
8	A	
9	D	
10	C	
11	D	Outside shape moves quarter turn to left. Inside shape changes.
12	D	Square turns 1/4 turn to left. Colors are flipped.
13	B	
14	C	In top row, the shape's sides increase by 1. In bottom row, the points of the star increase by 1.
15	A	
16	B	
17	C	
18	D	In top row, 3 small black triangles become 2 triangles (1 large black triangle & 1 medium white inner triangle). Large white squares get smaller (but stay same amount & same color). In bottom row, 3 small white squares become large white outer square & medium black inner square. Larger black circles get smaller but stay the same amount (3 circles) & same color (black).

CogAT® Quantitative Battery Answers

Number	Answer	Explanation
		Number Analogies
1	D	2 items (flowers) were added to top row. 2 items (bees) must be added to bottom row, which adds up to 5 bees.
2	A	One item was added to top row. One item (circle) must be added to bottom row, which adds up to 4 circles.
3	D	
4	A	2 items were added to top row. 2 items (penguins) must be added to bottom row, which adds up to 8 penguins.
5	B	
6	D	3 items were added to top row. 3 items (submarines) must be added to bottom row, which adds up to 8 submarines
7	A	3 items were subtracted from top row. 3 items (bananas) must be subtracted from bottom row, leaving 4 bananas.
8	C	3 items were subtracted from top row. 3 items (moons) must be subtracted from bottom row, leaving 5 moons.
9	B	
10	D	
11	D	
12	C	
13	B	
14	B	
15	A	
16	B	4 items were added to top row. 4 items (donuts) must be added to bottom row, which adds up to 4 donuts.
17	D	1.5 items were added to top row. 1.5 items (squares) must be added to bottom row, which adds up to 6 squares.
18	C	3 items were subtracted from top row. 3 items (arrows) must be subtracted from bottom row, leaving 1 arrow.

CogAT® Bubble Sheet

Use a No. 2 Pencil
Fill in bubble completely.
Ⓐ ● Ⓒ Ⓓ

Name:_____ Date:_____

1. Ⓐ Ⓑ Ⓒ Ⓓ	1. Ⓐ Ⓑ Ⓒ Ⓓ	1. Ⓐ Ⓑ Ⓒ Ⓓ
2. Ⓐ Ⓑ Ⓒ Ⓓ	2. Ⓐ Ⓑ Ⓒ Ⓓ	2. Ⓐ Ⓑ Ⓒ Ⓓ
3. Ⓐ Ⓑ Ⓒ Ⓓ	3. Ⓐ Ⓑ Ⓒ Ⓓ	3. Ⓐ Ⓑ Ⓒ Ⓓ
4. Ⓐ Ⓑ Ⓒ Ⓓ	4. Ⓐ Ⓑ Ⓒ Ⓓ	4. Ⓐ Ⓑ Ⓒ Ⓓ
5. Ⓐ Ⓑ Ⓒ Ⓓ	5. Ⓐ Ⓑ Ⓒ Ⓓ	5. Ⓐ Ⓑ Ⓒ Ⓓ
6. Ⓐ Ⓑ Ⓒ Ⓓ	6. Ⓐ Ⓑ Ⓒ Ⓓ	6. Ⓐ Ⓑ Ⓒ Ⓓ
7. Ⓐ Ⓑ Ⓒ Ⓓ	7. Ⓐ Ⓑ Ⓒ Ⓓ	7. Ⓐ Ⓑ Ⓒ Ⓓ
8. Ⓐ Ⓑ Ⓒ Ⓓ	8. Ⓐ Ⓑ Ⓒ Ⓓ	8. Ⓐ Ⓑ Ⓒ Ⓓ
9. Ⓐ Ⓑ Ⓒ Ⓓ	9. Ⓐ Ⓑ Ⓒ Ⓓ	9. Ⓐ Ⓑ Ⓒ Ⓓ
10. Ⓐ Ⓑ Ⓒ Ⓓ	10. Ⓐ Ⓑ Ⓒ Ⓓ	10. Ⓐ Ⓑ Ⓒ Ⓓ
11. Ⓐ Ⓑ Ⓒ Ⓓ	11. Ⓐ Ⓑ Ⓒ Ⓓ	11. Ⓐ Ⓑ Ⓒ Ⓓ
12. Ⓐ Ⓑ Ⓒ Ⓓ	12. Ⓐ Ⓑ Ⓒ Ⓓ	12. Ⓐ Ⓑ Ⓒ Ⓓ
13. Ⓐ Ⓑ Ⓒ Ⓓ	13. Ⓐ Ⓑ Ⓒ Ⓓ	13. Ⓐ Ⓑ Ⓒ Ⓓ
14. Ⓐ Ⓑ Ⓒ Ⓓ	14. Ⓐ Ⓑ Ⓒ Ⓓ	14. Ⓐ Ⓑ Ⓒ Ⓓ
15. Ⓐ Ⓑ Ⓒ Ⓓ	15. Ⓐ Ⓑ Ⓒ Ⓓ	15. Ⓐ Ⓑ Ⓒ Ⓓ
16. Ⓐ Ⓑ Ⓒ Ⓓ	16. Ⓐ Ⓑ Ⓒ Ⓓ	16. Ⓐ Ⓑ Ⓒ Ⓓ
17. Ⓐ Ⓑ Ⓒ Ⓓ	17. Ⓐ Ⓑ Ⓒ Ⓓ	17. Ⓐ Ⓑ Ⓒ Ⓓ
18. Ⓐ Ⓑ Ⓒ Ⓓ	18. Ⓐ Ⓑ Ⓒ Ⓓ	18. Ⓐ Ⓑ Ⓒ Ⓓ

BONUS

CHALLENGE
PRACTICE QUESTIONS

Includes questions from **ALL** batteries
-verbal, quantitative & non-verbal-
of the

CogAT FORM 7/8 - Grade 2

Please visit
https://originstutoring.lpages.co/
cogat-8-challenge-questions/
to access the challenge questions now!

a b c d

Made in the USA
Coppell, TX
27 October 2019